Protecting
the People of the Arrow

Written by Scott Wallace and
Kerrie Shanahan

Photography by Scott Wallace

Flying Start
to Literacy®

CONTENTS

INTRODUCTION

In remote places in different parts of the world live small communities of people who have no contact with the outside world. They do not have phones, the Internet, electricity or cars. They don't have money or shops in which to buy food. They don't have schools to learn in, or doctors to perform surgeries in hospitals.

These groups of people are known as "uncontacted people".

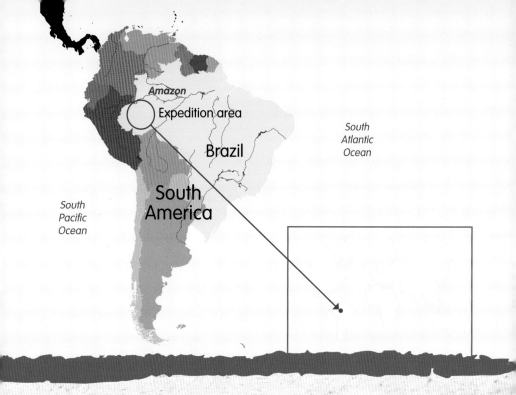

A group of uncontacted people, known as the People of the Arrow, live deep in the Amazon Rainforest in Brazil. This book is about a three-month expedition to find out the extent of their **seasonal treks** so that they could be protected from the outside world and continue to live in their traditional ways.

Sydney Possuelo, an **activist** from Brazil, led the dangerous and ambitious mission. American journalist Scott Wallace joined the expedition and documented this adventure so that the rest of the world could learn about the People of the Arrow. In this book, you will see many of Scott's photos from this epic journey.

Chapter 1

AN EXPEDITION IS PLANNED

THE PEOPLE OF THE ARROW

Deep in the Amazon Rainforest, live a group of people known as the People of the Arrow, or **Flecheiros**. Not much is known about them. What language do they speak? Do they even have a name for themselves?

There are stories about these people shooting poisoned arrows at anyone who gets too close, so we assume they are protective of their home.

Most experts agree that "no contact" is the best way to protect these people. But without knowing the limits of where they move on their **seasonal treks**, can officials fully protect their land? How could "outsiders" be kept away?

Approximately 80 uncontacted tribes live in the Amazon Rainforest. They live in remote places that are difficult to reach.

In 2002, an expedition to find the People of the Arrow was planned. Brazilian explorer and **activist** Sydney Possuelo led the expedition, and he gathered his team of mostly **indigenous** men who knew the Amazon jungle well.

Brazilian explorer and activist Sydney Possuelo

WHO IS SYDNEY POSSUELO?

He is an expert on remote tribes.

In the early years of his work, Sydney's job was to locate and make nonviolent contact with isolated tribes.

These people could then be "helped" by providing them with food, medicines and other supplies.

Over time, Sydney saw the negative effects that "contact" had on these people – they included loss of land, language and **identity**:

"Once you make contact, you start to destroy their universe."

Sydney fought for change and, eventually, a new law was made in 1988. It became **illegal** to contact remote tribes living in Brazil.

Sydney continued locating remote tribes but without making contact.

The aims of this mission were to find proof these remote tribes existed and to find the boundaries of the land they occupied. The team would also check if there were any threats to their well-being. And most importantly, they would attempt to do this without any contact.

Sydney had to be well prepared. He mapped out the route the expedition would take by flying over the area in a helicopter. Food, water and other supplies were prepared, and transport was arranged.

Sydney knew the trip would be a challenge. The forest was extremely thick, and in some parts, it was almost impossible to pass through. There were no roads or air strips. If anyone on the expedition was injured, there was no way of getting help quickly.

But Sydney loved challenges.

Chapter 2

DISCOVERIES ARE MADE

THE JOURNEY BEGINS

Sydney and his team began their journey by boat. They travelled up the Itaquai River, a branch of the famous Amazon River. They passed through several villages on either side of the riverbanks. The further they went, the fewer people they saw – and the thicker the jungle became.

After about three weeks, they reached the point where they needed to travel inland to find the People of the Arrow. They could go no further by boat. It was time to walk!

The expedition's boats move upriver.

TREKKING THROUGH THE JUNGLE

They fought their way through thick jungle. They waded through streams or used fallen trees as bridges. The trek was steamy and hot, and the humidity made it difficult to breathe.

The trees were massive, with a high canopy that let hardly any light through. The sounds of monkeys hooting, birds squawking and insects chirping filled the air.

> "It felt as though we were walking on the bottom of the ocean."
> *—Journalist Scott Wallace*

The journey was risky. Lurking in the forest was dangerous wildlife such as jaguars, snakes and poisonous frogs. And there was always the threat of being attacked by the People of the Arrow defending their homeland. Trekking through the dense jungle, the whole team was extremely watchful.

A jungle home
Remote Brazilian tribes are self-sufficient. They use the forest and its resources to meet all their needs, such as food, shelter and medicines.

A jaguar

13

The expedition set up camp.

EVIDENCE

Days and nights passed. There were days of walking and nights of setting up camp, cooking and eating, and sleeping in hammocks. Eventually, they saw traces of the People of the Arrow!

They came across an empty campsite in a clearing, with a couple of small, abandoned huts made of dry grasses. Sydney guessed it was a fishing camp that was used for short periods of time to stock up on fresh fish.

A clay pot and a small cage made of sticks were left in the middle of the empty camp. Sydney knew this camp had not been used for some time. It was likely they were still a safe distance away from the home of the People of the Arrow.

The team members were excited to see this evidence of life. They headed off, and before long, they came across a new discovery . . . footprints!

Shelter
Remote tribes clear the thick forest to make their settlements. They use bark, branches, leaves and grasses from the forest to build their homes.

A SIGHTING

Sydney examined the footprints. They were fresh! He knew the owner of these prints had taken off in a hurry and was probably close by.

Sydney asked everyone to be quiet. They were all on high alert. They scanned the jungle but saw nothing. Then a couple of Sydney's team members saw the backs of two people as they sprinted off into the thick jungle and disappeared.

This was exciting! But at the same time, it was frightening. The People of the Arrow knew they were nearby!

Would the tribe use poisoned arrows to defend their home? Were Sydney and his team being watched? Were the People of the Arrow about to attack?

Weapons

Some remote tribes make poison called **curare** by boiling various plants. They put the curare on the tips of their arrows and spears to use for hunting and to defend themselves. Some tribes have guns and axes that they have traded with other neighbouring tribes that have been in contact with outsiders.

Darts poisoned with curare

Chapter 3

DANGER!

A WARNING

Sydney's team continued on its mission. After two days of trekking, they reached a path – and they could tell it was used regularly. This was an obvious sign that they were close to a permanent settlement.

They followed the path for a short time until they reached a small tree branch that had been recently snapped so that it hung across the path. For an experienced explorer like Sydney, this was a clear warning sign. He knew exactly what it meant:

"This is **universal** language in the jungle. It means: 'Stay out. Go no further.'"

Food
Remote tribes get their food by hunting animals, fishing, growing crops and gathering foods such as wild berries, fruits and nuts.

Breaking camp

Sydney had seen enough – he had evidence. He knew this was the home of the People of the Arrow. Now, it was time to leave these people alone and to get his team safely home.

The team turned off the path, bypassing the place where the People of the Arrow lived.

LOST!

Sydney and his team came to a clearing and stopped to rest. At this point, they realised that two members of the group were missing. This was not a good place to be lost.

They waited for the two lost men to return, but there was no sign of them. Sydney sent out a search party.

Again, they waited. The two men did not return, and by then, the search party had been gone for a long time, too. Eventually, Sydney sent a larger group to search for everyone who was missing.

A **scout** on the expedition

Finally both search groups returned but without the two lost men. They did, however, have some news. They had found the lost men's shoe prints on the path, past the broken-branch barrier. They had also followed the prints along the track until they saw an amazing sight – a whole village.

Medicines

Remote tribes use plants, fruits, vines and parts of animals to create their own medicines to treat illnesses and injuries. Uncontacted people have never been exposed to diseases that are common for most humans, and they therefore have no immunity and no treatments for them. Measles, the flu or even a cold could kill them.

For body painting, sunscreen and insect repellent

Root used for toothaches, cuts and bruises

For sore throats and coughs

For mouth ulcers

THE VILLAGE

The search parties reported on what they had seen.

The village had 14 large huts and a massive garden with plants including sugarcane and papaya. Campfires were glowing – some with caterpillars roasting on them. There were piles of meat ready to be cooked. It looked like the people were about to prepare a big feast, perhaps a celebration? But something had startled the villagers, and they had left in a hurry.

Several masks made out of bark rested next to big bowls of red dye that could be used as body paint. And hidden under some leaves were two big bowls of poison being brewed – poison to be used on the tips of the villagers' arrows!

Tribal life

Remote tribes have celebrations and customs. These involve special foods, dancing and storytelling. Some tribes wear masks and paint their faces and bodies for special ceremonies. They also have ways of making sure people do the right thing and follow the tribe's rules.

Papaya trees are native to the northern part of South America.

Sydney and the rest of the group were amazed – this was a clear snapshot of how the People of the Arrow live.

But where were their two missing friends? Were they hurt? Had they been killed by the People of the Arrow?

Sadly, they could not wait any longer to find out – it was time for Sydney and his team to leave.

Chapter 4

RETREAT!

TIME TO GO

Sydney knew he and his team had to get out of there quickly. The People of the Arrow could be hiding in the jungle, planning an attack.

As they packed up, one of Sydney's most trusted men wanted to try once more to find the missing men. Sydney agreed but warned him to be careful. He didn't want to lose any more men.

Matis, an **indigenous** scout on the expedition

Luckily, the **scout**, named Matis, found new shoe prints, which he followed. The two men were found – they were scared but unhurt.

The missing men were sorry for leaving the group. They admitted that they had gone past the broken tree branch that was a warning to stop; they just wanted to see what was there. After walking through the village, they panicked. They left the path and ran through the jungle.

They were lucky to be found. And it was fortunate the People of the Arrow had not been the ones to find them.

HEADING HOME

Now that the whole group was safe again, Sydney reminded his team of the importance of sticking to the no-contact philosophy. If the People of the Arrow had welcomed the two missing men, it could have been disastrous for their tribe. The outsiders could have passed on germs that could kill these people.

Sydney and his group headed off on the long trek home. Would they make it out of the jungle safely? They weren't sure, but they knew they had to move quickly. They walked for three days, almost without stopping. They were exhausted, tired and hungry, but they had to keep moving.

Finally, they reached the river. The only way out from there was by boat. They didn't have boats, so they would have to make some.

Sydney and the group set up camp and began to build canoes. They used trees and traditional techniques to make two large canoes that could transport all members of the team.

Building a dugout canoe

The explorers began paddling. They paddled all day long for a week or so until they were close enough to reach the outside world with their radio. They used the radio to organise a place on the river where it was deep enough for a larger boat to meet them. They then paddled for yet another full week until they reached the meeting point.

The larger boat took the tired explorers back to where their journey began. After almost three months, they were home safely. What an adventure!

So what did they achieve?

Paddling downstream in a dugout canoe

The expedition was deemed a success. It produced evidence that the People of the Arrow existed and that they were living safely and successfully. The area where they lived could be fully protected from outside contact.

Sydney summed up the trip:

"Here the People of the Arrow are living well. They hunt, they fish, they grow food. They must be healthy. . . . They have feasts. They are happy. They don't ask anything from the white man. They don't need us!"

This was the first time that outsiders had visited this remote place. Would it be the last?

CONCLUSION

Uncontacted people like the People of the Arrow are unique and interesting, and many of us would like to know more about them. We understand, however, it is dangerous for them to be contacted.

Activists such as Sydney are working to make sure that the rest of the world leaves uncontacted people alone. These people have the right to live safely in their homes, just as we do.

Sydney Possuelo

GLOSSARY

activist a person who helps make changes; they take action to help change laws

curare a type of poison that is made from the bark of some South American plants

Flecheiros a group of uncontacted people that live in a region of the Amazon jungle in South America

identity the beliefs and ideas that make a particular person or group different from others

illegal something that is prohibited by law

indigenous living in a particular area; having a strong connection with a place over a long period of time

scout a person who is sent to find out information

seasonal treks movements that happen during a particular time of year, following the seasons

universal something that everyone experiences and understands, even if they don't speak the same language or come from the same group

INDEX